Shakespeare
On Golf

"What sport shall we devise here in this garden
To drive away the heavy thought of care?"

—RICHARD II, III, iv, 1–2

Shakespeare On Golf

WIT AND WISDOM FROM
THE GREAT ELIZABETHAN GOLFER
AND POET

John Tullius
and Joe Ortiz

Illustrations by Harry Trumbore

HYPERION

New York

Library of Congress Cataloging-in-Publication Data
Tullius, John
Shakespeare on Golf: wit and wisdom from the great Elizabethan golfer and
poet/ John Tullius and Joe Ortiz: illustrations by Harry Trumbore.—1st ed.
p.   cm.
ISBN 0-7868-6320-X
2. Golf—Miscellanea. 2. Shakespeare, William, 1564-1616—Quotations.
I. Ortiz, Joe, 1946-   . II. Title.
GV967.T83   1997
796.352—dc21   97-17609
CIP

Book design by Jennifer Ann Daddio

FIRST EDITION

10 8 6 4 2 1 3 5 7 9

Introduction

Shakespeare on Golf is the long-lost compendium of golfing wit and wisdom from one of mankind's greatest sporting minds. It was a closely kept secret that Shakespeare's day job was head pro at the Stratford-on-Avon Links, Croquet, and Swim Club, where such luminaries as Christopher "You da Man" Marlowe and Francis "Boom Boom" Bacon were members and fellow touring pros.

For centuries a cabal of college professors have deliberately concealed the truth about Shakespeare with their vacuous drivel about metaphors and alliteration. You remember those Nightol lectures in World Lit. 101 about "The Symbolic Use of Color in Richard III" or "The Monastic Tradition and the Falstaffian

<u>Welstraum</u> in the Henry VI Trilogy"? Of course you don't. That was the point. Anything to obscure the fact that the so-called greatest writer of all time, the playwright whose required course was driving your GPA ineluctably below 3.0 (thus keeping you from getting into a decent MBA program), was nothing more than a dimple-brained golf nut.

Just like you.

The truth is the teaching axioms of the Bard were literary fodder for his plays and poetry. Yes, indeed, before Harvey Pennick's little red blockbuster there was William Shakespeare's <u>Let Me Count the Strokes: Eighteen Stanzas to a Better Golf Game</u>. But alas, poor Yorick, that teed-up treasure, that alliterative love sonnet to links lore and legend, that love's labour was lost for over three centuries. Lost, that is, until Joe Ortiz and I happened upon a crumbling, spike-marked quarto in the shoe pocket of a golf bag in the closet of a London brothel (don't ask!) and discovered the soul-liberating truth that Shakespeare was first and foremost history's finest golf instructor.

So, sit back golf lovers everywhere, and drink

in the true wisdom of the Bard. You will be as amazed and inspired as we were by the invaluable tips that abound, and you'll realize why Shakespeare has been around almost as long as the game itself.

John Tullius
Wailea, Blue Course
7:32 Tee Time: MWF

Acknowledgments

To Gayle and Shannon—
thanks for letting us tee off

Foreword:
Hamlet's Lunacy

It wasn't so much that Uncle Claude bludgeoned Daddy and bedded Mummy that drove gentle Hamlet to prune half of Denmark's royal tree. No, it was his moody swings that made him lose grip. He exited the scene of his last humiliation, then lost his surething bird to water, after jacknifing Polonius, his sometime driver "behind a curtain of birch." Then it got ugly. On number five, he pulled a poisoned iron—and all Denmark shook with grief.

*"What a hell of witchcraft lies
In the small orb. . ."*

—<u>A LOVER'S COMPLAINT</u>, 288

"Alas, poor duke! The task he undertakes
Is numb'ring sands and drinking oceans dry."

—<u>RICHARD II</u>, II, ii, 145–146

"I have found
The very cause of Hamlet's lunacy."

—<u>HAMLET</u>, II, ii, 48–49

Shakespeare
On Golf

Lesson One:
The Swing

". . .There's not the smallest orb which thou behold'st
But in his motion like an angel sings. . . "
—<u>THE MERCHANT OF VENICE</u>, V, i, 60–61

One of Shakespeare's greatest talents was the ability to use rhythm and tempo to add power and finesse to his play. From the iambic pentameter of his measured opening to the <u>deus ex machina</u> of his downbeat, Will's delivery was a show-stopper. That dramatic pause at the top, awaiting only the "thunderlike percussion" of his tigerish bomblasts. There he'd stand after one of his trademark big finishes—the hero of those classic hits, motionless at centerstage, head still bowed, arms raised above his head. . .

I. Correcting the Flying Elbow

"O, then how quickly should this arm of
    mine,
Now prisoner to the palsy, chastise thee,
And minister correction to thy fault."

—<u>RICHARD II</u>, II, iii, 103–105

II. The Key to Power Is the Left Hand

*"the greater throw
May turn by fortune from the weaker
hand."*

—<u>THE MERCHANT OF VENICE</u>, II, i, 33–34

Lesson Two:
Teeing It Up

"Like a new-kill'd bird she trembling lies"

—THE RAPE OF LUCRECE, 457

Shakespeare has been called the world's premier playmaker. Left to right, right to left, English or Hebrew, man, could he manipulate that old globe. Nary a wasted movement in the works neither. Just silk and greasepaint that packed a wallop. But Will wasn't all Et tu, Brutus, all course de grâce. He had the feel of Romeo whenever he approached that chaste ground. In fact, the nearer he drew to "the hole of discretion . . . whose unear'd womb disdains the tillage of thy husbandry," the more seductive his caress.

I. The Driver

"Strike, as thou didst at Caesar."

—<u>JULIUS CAESAR</u>, IV, iii, 105

"make you ready your stiff bats and
   clubs.
Rome and her rats are at the point of
   battle."

—CORIOLANUS, I, i, 165–166

"The woods are ruthless, dreadful, deaf, and dull;
There speak, and strike, brave boys, and take your turns."

—<u>TITUS ANDRONICUS</u>, II, i, 128–129

II. Iron Play and Approach Shots

"Friar John, go hence;
Get me an iron . . . ."

—<u>ROMEO AND JULIET</u>, V, ii, 20–21

"The mellow plum doth fall, the green sticks fast."

—<u>VENUS AND ADONIS</u>, 527–528

III. Pitching and Chipping

"And what a pitch she flew above the
    rest!
To see how God in all His creatures
    works!
Yea, man and birds are fain of climbing
    high."

—<u>HENRY VI, PART 2</u>, II, i, 6–8

*"they would change their state
And situation with those dancing chips"*

—<u>SONNET CXXVIII</u>

"I cannot bound a pitch above dull woe."

—<u>ROMEO AND JULIET</u>, I, iv, 21

IV. Sandplay

"... like a fairy trip upon the green,
Or like a nymph, with long dishevell'd hair,
Dance on the sands ..."

—<u>VENUS AND ADONIS</u>, 146–148

"Alack, sir, I am sand-blind; I know you not."

—<u>MERCHANT OF VENICE</u>, II, ii, 77

"The earth hath swallow'd all my hopes . . ."

—ROMEO AND JULIET, I, ii, 14

"God and your Majesty
Protect mine innocence, or I fall into
The trap is laid for me!"

—<u>HENRY VIII</u>, V, i, 140–142

Lesson Three:
The Putter

"Every man put[t] himself into triumph"

—<u>OTHELLO</u>, II, ii, 4

Perhaps no man understood the putter like Shakespeare, just as no man understood love like him. He often remarked that putting was a marriage of inconvenience between the hands and the shaft. Squeeze the rod lightly as you stroke the ball, he'd counsel, "until the bell rings and the widow weeps."

He was a master of the four-foot beast which, of course, is where most men go limp from nerves. Never up, never in, Will would say. Then he'd take aim and just ram it home.

Marlowe had the privilege of going out with Shakespeare many times and watching Will's magic wand at work. Oh, how Willy could pick up those birds! Once he lined her up, it was strictly Wham, bam! Thank you, Lady Macbeth!

I. Dealing with the Yips

"Cold fearful drops stand on my trembling flesh.
What! Do I fear myself? There's none else by."

—<u>RICHARD III</u>, V, iii, 181–182

". . .Green, thou art the midwife of my woe."

—<u>RICHARD II</u>, II, ii, 62

II. Reading the Greens

*"O, pardon me that I descend so low
To show the line and the predicament"*

—<u>HENRY IV, PART 1</u>, I, iii, 167–168

"Toward London they all bend their course."

—<u>RICHARD III</u>, IV, v, 17

III. Uphill, Downhill

"Let go thy hold when a great wheel runs down a hill, lest it break thy neck with following; but the great one that goes upward, let him draw thee after."

—KING LEAR, II, iv, 72–75

Lesson Four:
Specialty Shots

*"I chose an eagle,
And did avoid a puttock."*

—<u>CYMBELINE</u>, I, i, 139

Shakespeare had a special affinity for the odd-ball. Witness that cross-dressing number in <u>As You Like It</u>, or those damned fairies that kept popping up every time he played a round at Maypole. Or how about that "course unnatural" in Denmark, haunted by a ghost? The place had a shared green so two players could putt out at the same time. creating a play within a play.

Truth is, the Bard was a master on hardwood or hardpan. The more troublesome his play, the nobler his character, the subtler his stroke. His pearls flew across those trap-filled plots, singing through scores of timbre, eluding high-born ruffs, until they rolled like dimpled moons into those four-inch-round periods.

I. Hitting Over Water

"Now would I give a thousand furlongs of sea for an acre of barren ground, long heath, brown furze, anything. The wills above be done! But I would fain die a dry death."

—THE TEMPEST, I, i, 69–72

*"A cunning man did calculate my birth
And told me that by water I should die."*

—<u>HENRY VI, PART 2</u>, IV, i, 34–35

"Alas! The seas hath cast me on the
   rocks,
Wash'd me from shore to shore, and left
   me breath
Nothing to think on but ensuing death."

—<u>PERICLES</u>, II, i, 6–7

"Glory is like a circle in the water . . .
Which never ceaseth to enlarge itself,
Till by broad spreading it disperse to
   nought."

—HENRY VI, PART 1, I, ii, 133

II. Hacking Your Way Out
of the Rough

"I have been studying how I may compare
This prison where I live unto the World
And for because the World is populous,
And here is not a creature but myself,
I cannot do it; yet I'll hammer it out."

—<u>RICHARD II</u>, V, v, 1–4

"a lie, an odious, damned lie;
Upon my soul, a lie, a wicked lie."

—<u>OTHELLO</u>, V, ii, 180–181

III. Cutting the Dogleg

"Why *dost thou run so many mile about*
When thou mayst tell thy tale a nearer
    way?"

—<u>RICHARD III</u>, IV, iv, 461–462

IV. Left to Right, Right to Left—Whatever!

"Slice, I say! . . . Slice! that's my humor."

—<u>MERRY WIVES OF WINDSOR</u>, I, i, 135

V. Chili-Dips, Duckhooks, and Divots

"Foul devil, for God's sake, hence, and
    trouble us not;
For thou hast made the happy earth
    thy hell,
Fill'd it with cursing cries and deep
    exclaims."

—RICHARD III, I, ii, 50–52

*"If thou delight to view thy heinous deeds
Behold this pattern of thy butcheries."*

—<u>RICHARD III</u>, I, ii, 53–54

Lesson Five:
Coach Will's Surefire
Stroke Savers

"Superfluous branches
We lop away, that bearing bows may live."

—<u>RICHARD II</u>, III, iv, 63–64

It's true that Shakespeare had a dark side. A side that reared its ugly clubhead whenever the Bard, for instance, found his ball playing footsie with an O.B. stake. (Followed quickly by Will playing footsie with his ball.) Like Shylock, he was a genius at improving his lie. Every time he found his lost ball, it had a clear view to the green and an anthill for a tee. And as to thigh-high rough and low-hanging limbs, Will simply cut the offenders down to size with a keenly sharpened sand-wedge. He once prophesized he could make "Birnam Wood remove to Dunsinane." And quicker than you could quoth Banquo, a stand of chopped saplings appeared before him.

Will was most shameless on the green, however. Like Caesar, you could never trust his mark. Every time he picked up his ha'penny, his ball was three inches closer to the hole.

I. Lining up Your Putt

*"Can you nominate in order now
the degrees of the lie?"*

—<u>AS YOU LIKE IT</u>, V, iv, 93–94

11. What O.B. Stakes?

"If you will take a homely man's advice,
Be not found here."

—<u>MACBETH</u>, IV, ii, 68–69

"Stones have been known to move and trees to speak"

—<u>MACBETH</u>, III, iv, 123

III. How to "Find" Your Lost Ball (without Getting Caught)

*"O, thus I found her, straying in the park,
Seeking to hide herself."*

—<u>TITUS ANDRONICUS</u>, III, i, 88

"I found him under a tree, like a dropp'd acorn."

—<u>AS YOU LIKE IT</u>, III, ii, 248

IV. Fixing a Ball Mark

"Out, damned spot! out, I say!"

—<u>MACBETH</u>, V, i, 39

V. Talking to the Ball

"Work you, then . . . .
Hang cur! hang . . . "

—<u>THE TEMPEST</u>, I, i, 45–46

"Betwixt thy begging and my meditation.
I am not in the giving vein to-day."

—<u>RICHARD III</u>, IV, ii, 118–119

Lesson Six:
Picking the Right
Equipment

"Out of a great deal of old iron I chose forth."

—<u>HENRY VI, PART 1</u>, I, ii, 101

To Shakespeare, matching a player to the right equipment meant a marriage of true minds. Of course, it also meant his cut of sales at the pro shop. His favorite game was to bring a new club out to the range for his eager students to ogle. One day it was his Cymbeline-of-sight putter, the next it was his Falstaff "Fat Belly" driver. On Saturday he'd show off his Richard III humpback sand-wedge; Sunday it was his own line of clubs, Shakespeare's As You Like It irons.

He'd let these poor unsuspecting get a feel for his pricey sticks, before snatching them away as if they were a secret best kept. Then, with a little disdainful shake of the head, he'd offer up his sales coup de grâce. "You shall be a woodmonger, and buy nothing of me but cudgels." Next thing you know, there they'd be, ringing up the abacus in the Pound o' Flesh Pro Shop.

I. The Real Golfer Always Blames His Equipment

"they . . . put a barren scepter in my gripe"

—<u>MACBETH</u>, III, i, 62

II. Accursed Course
Designers and Their
Accursed Courses

"This is as strange a maze as e'er men trod."

—<u>THE TEMPEST</u>, V, ii, 242

"Fie, what an indirect and peevish course"

—<u>RICHARD III</u>, III, i, 31

"O! cursed be the hand that made these holes!
Cursed the heart that had the heart to do it!"

—RICHARD III, I, ii, 14–15

Lesson Seven:
Nobler of Mind—
The Mental Game

"Moderate lamentation is the right of the dead, excessive grief the enemy to the living."

—<u>ALL'S WELL THAT ENDS WELL</u>, I, i, 64–65

The mental game was not Shakespeare's forte. To be frank, he had a tendency to overthink just about everything. "To be or not to be." That kind of stuff is suicide to a golfer. "Grippe it and rip it!" Bacon used to scream in exasperation. Some historians have suggested, in fact, that when the Bard agonized too long over his next attempt, Sir Francis would sometimes snatch the stick from Will and finish the play for him.

I. Keeping a Positive
Mental Attitude

"Things past redress are now with me past care."

—<u>RICHARD II</u>, II, iii, 171

II. "You Da Man"—
Confidence Breeds Success

". . . his codpiece seems as massy as his club"

—<u>MUCH ADO ABOUT NOTHING</u>, III, iii, 146–147

"I will awe him with my cudgel; it shall hang like a meteor o'er the cuckhold's horns."

—<u>MERRY WIVES OF WINDSOR</u>, II, ii, 291–292

III. Hitting It Stiff— Risk and Reward

"a garish flag
To be the aim of every dangerous shot"

—<u>RICHARD III</u>, IV, iv, 88–89

IV. Trash Talking and Psych Jobbing ("praises sauc'd with lies"—<u>Coriolanus</u>, I, ix, 53)

"How long hast thou been a grave-maker?"

—<u>HAMLET</u>, V, i, 153

"This proves that thou canst not read."

—<u>THE TWO GENTLEMEN OF VERONA</u>, III, i, 297–298

"Spit in the hole, man, and tune again."

—<u>THE TAMING OF THE SHREW</u>, III, i, 40

"Have you a mind to sink?"

—<u>THE TEMPEST</u>, I, i, 41–42

Lesson Eight:
Requiem for a Golf
Widow—The 19th Hole

"I would give all my fame for a pot of ale and safety."

—<u>HENRY V</u>, III, ii, 14

Shakespeare knew well the dual raison d'être of golf—drinking and gambling. In fact, Will was fond of repeating great Falstaff's slurred axiom: "If these blinking courses would only install brothels in the clubhouse, golf would have man's three major vices rolled into one beautiful game."

"Score a pint of Bastard in the Half-Moon," they'd all yell if someone sank a hole-winning putt. Then onto the next tee and the next brew, till fair Denmark loomed in their blank eyes.

I. Sandbagging for Fun and Profit

"The true prince may, for recreation
    sake,
prove a false thief."

—<u>HENRY IV, PART 1</u>, I, ii, 173–174

II. The Postmortem
in the Bar

"All shall eat and drink on my score"

—<u>HENRY VI, PART 2</u>, IV, ii, 80

About the Authors

Joe Ortiz is the co-owner of Gayle's Bakery and Rosticceria in Capitola, California. He is the co-author of <u>The Village Baker's Wife</u> and <u>Kitchen Beds and Garden Tables—Natural Ways to Grow and Cook Vegetables</u>. He has also written for <u>Bon Appétit</u>, <u>Food & Wine</u>, and for <u>Cooks Illustrated</u>. Joe is a 14 handicap golfer who has safely shot "under his body temperature (98.6)" at courses like Augusta National, Cypress Point, Pebble Beach, and Olympic Club.

John Tullius is Director of the Maui Writers Conference. He is also the author of twelve books, including co-authoring the best-seller <u>Body of a Crime</u> and <u>Against the Law</u>. He has also written for <u>Cosmopolitan</u>, <u>Playboy</u>, and <u>Town and Country</u>, and was a contributing editor for <u>Tennis</u> magazine.

About the Illustrator

Harry Trumbore has illustrated over 25 books for both adults and children and has worked extensively in television and newspaper cartooning. His proudest achievement is a birdie on the 8th hole at Ballybunion. He lives in Maplewood, New Jersey.